THE CHRISTMAS PROMISE

PACKED WITH PUZZLES, MAZES AND MORE!

Art and activity book

Finish the picture by drawing lots and
lots of sparkly stars all over these pages!

the good book
for children

The Christmas Promise Art and Activity Book
© The Good Book Company 2015, reprinted 2017 (twice), 2018, 2019 (twice), 2020, 2021, 2022.

"The Good Book For Children" is an imprint of The Good Book Company Ltd.
thegoodbook.com | www.thegoodbook.co.uk
thegoodbook.com.au | thegoodbook.co.nz | thegoodbook.co.in

Design and illustration by André Parker, based on original illustrations by Catalina Echeverri

ISBN: 9781784980139 | Printed in India

A long, long time ago – so long that it's hard to imagine – God promised a new King. He would be a NEW KING; a RESCUING KING; a FOREVER KING!

Gabriel's maze

The Christmas story starts with an angel.
WHOOSH! He came from God to see Mary.

Can you help him find his way?

Joseph has a dream

Mary was going to marry Joseph,
so God sent another angel.

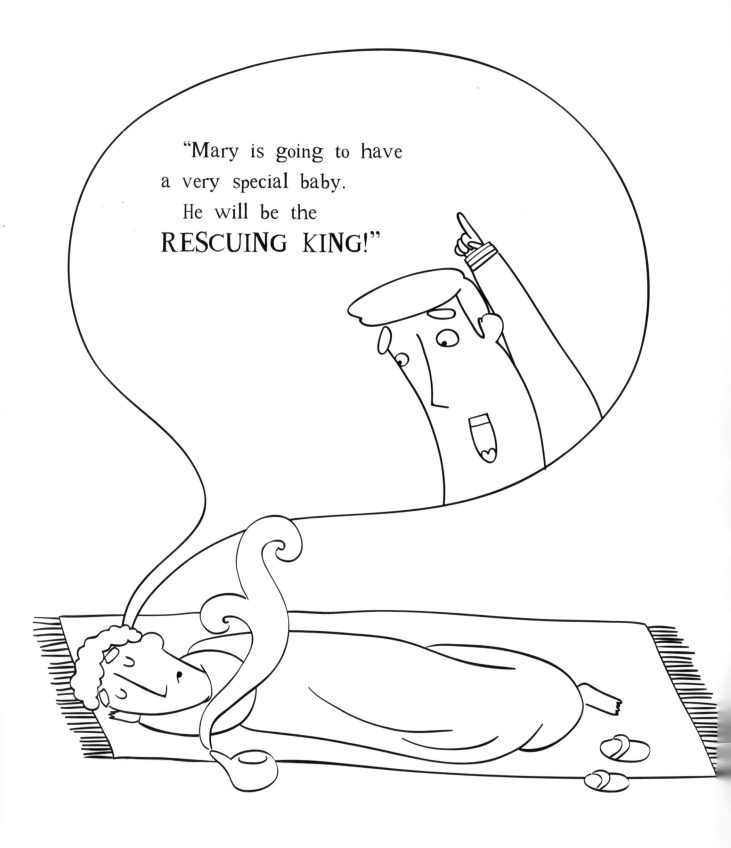

Wordsearch

h	K	i	g	b	h	r	e	s	c	u	e	j	h	u
m	e	s	s	a	g	e	f	r	z	a	i	e	r	r
e	k	i	j	u	f	t	r	h	b	j	l	o	e	b
u	y	p	m	a	r	y	e	s	l	K	o	v	n	v
y	h	r	d	e	s	w	s	b	g	a	e	o	p	t
h	e	o	i	n	a	K	l	a	a	r	t	v	c	b
j	g	m	s	a	w	n	z	o	o	b	i	u	g	K
y	o	i	i	b	h	p	i	f	l	y	y	r	d	a
l	K	s	u	t	o	p	e	l	e	K	i	d	h	w
a	l	e	e	w	o	t	a	q	a	v	x	c	u	n
i	j	l	f	p	s	u	n	s	z	t	b	m	h	o
c	i	o	p	h	h	b	g	r	h	f	a	v	K	s
e	t	r	b	m	l	o	e	g	j	t	i	c	i	i
p	b	y	d	r	e	p	l	l	y	u	f	g	n	l
s	u	e	d	r	e	a	m	v	e	x	i	o	g	a

☐ angel ☐ Joseph ☐ promise

☐ baby ☐ King ☐ rescue

☐ dream ☐ Mary ☐ special

☐ forever ☐ message ☐ whoosh

Going to Bethlehem

God had promised that his new King would be born in a little city called Bethlehem.

Finish the picture by drawing lots and lots
of houses and busy people!

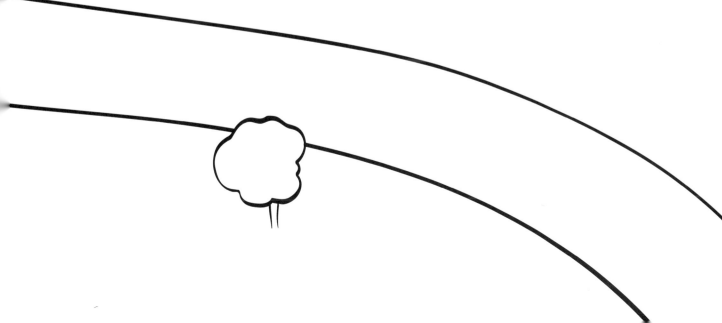

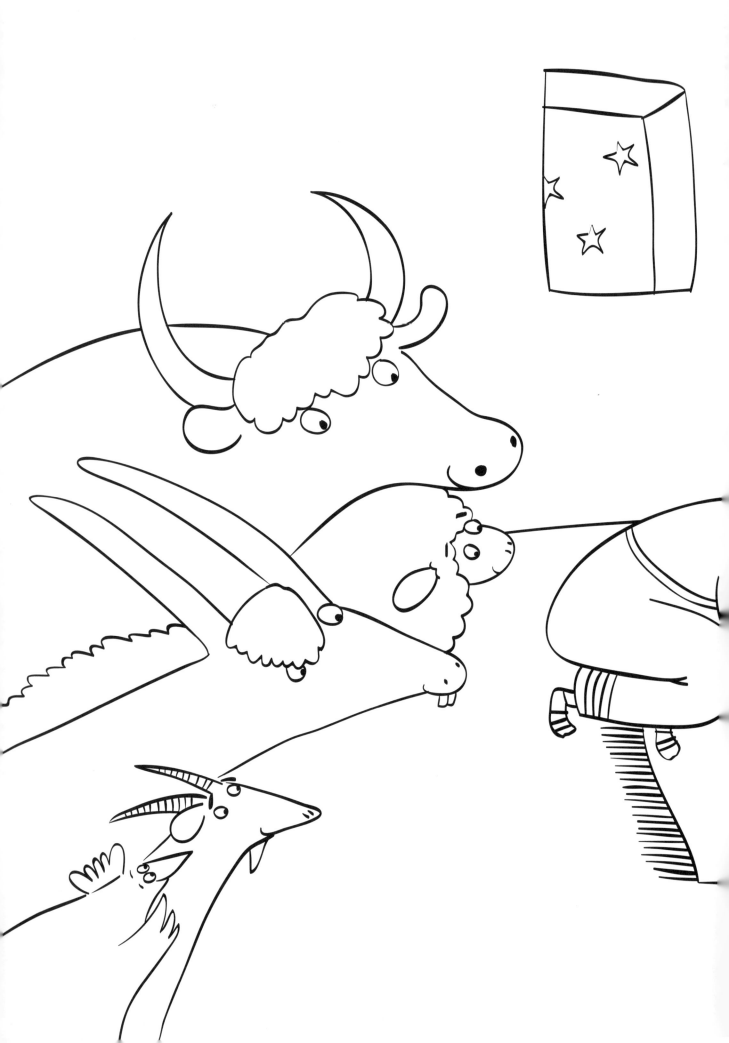

The King is born!

All the other mangers in Bethlehem held food
for hungry animals to munch.
But this manger held a tiny baby.

Join the dots

Start at number 1 and draw a line to each dot to see where God's special new King is sleeping!

Now decorate your picture!

The new King

Can you decorate this picture with lots of patterns?

The shepherds' surprise

Finish the picture by drawing lots of
sleepy sheep and shining stars!

"DON'T BE AFRAID!

I have wonderful good news for you!
God's chosen King has been born tonight!"

Help these angels celebrate by decorating them and
adding lots of twinkling stars to the sky!

The special star

Some wise men living far, far away
had also been sent a message...

Can you find the special star that the wise men saw? Match the star in the telescope to the one in the sky, then decorate the picture.

The wise men's journey

The wise men were so excited! So they went on a loooong journey to see the new King.

Draw a long wiggly path to Bethlehem, then finish the picture by adding lots of trees, animals and houses.

# Wordsearch

d	r	b	m	a	j	u	a	n	m	g	j	s	o	n
g	a	e	f	s	o	o	r	j	n	r	a	l	c	b
r	n	t	e	v	o	l	u	i	u	a	c	o	e	r
s	d	h	u	d	K	b	p	r	m	e	o	l	l	e
a	r	l	w	n	y	e	o	z	n	f	b	w	e	d
r	e	e	t	s	e	y	f	p	s	e	t	h	b	t
a	d	h	u	l	m	K	s	e	p	u	y	d	r	h
h	i	e	s	h	e	p	h	e	r	d	s	n	a	n
m	t	m	i	l	l	i	e	h	e	d	o	e	t	a
e	K	o	p	s	y	o	p	s	s	e	y	f	e	g
w	i	s	e	m	e	n	i	t	e	t	t	r	o	e
f	w	n	c	a	m	e	l	r	n	i	s	m	e	m
d	r	e	a	y	x	p	d	u	t	c	a	t	u	i
t	m	a	n	g	e	r	p	g	s	x	e	y	a	g
s	i	e	i	g	g	a	m	y	t	e	j	f	o	r

☐ Bethlehem   ☐ journey   ☐ shepherds

☐ camel   ☐ manger   ☐ sleeping

☐ celebrate   ☐ presents   ☐ star

☐ excited   ☐ sheep   ☐ wise men

The wise men visit Jesus

The greatest King

Everything God promised came true.
There are lots and lots of different Kings in the world, but God sent the greatest King of all!

Can you match these Kings to their shadows?

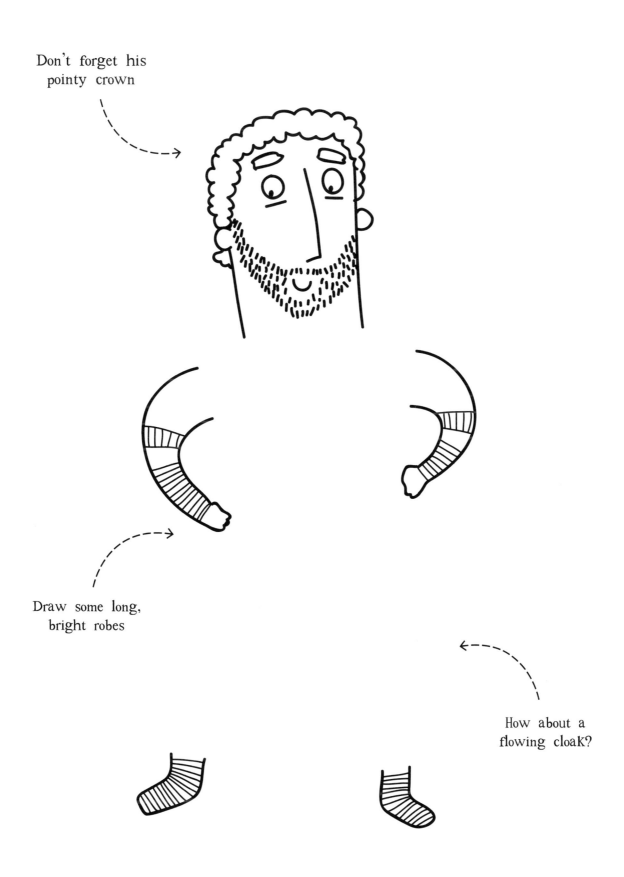

Don't forget his pointy crown

Draw some long, bright robes

How about a flowing cloak?

Finish this picture of the best King of all - King Jesus!

new King

Rescuing forever King

Answers

Gabriel's maze

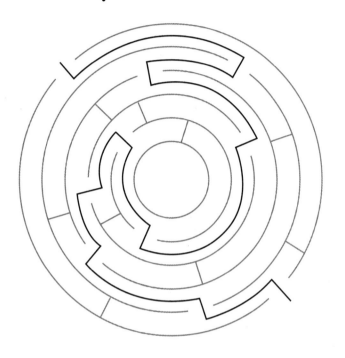

Wordsearch 1

h	K	i	g	b	h	r	e	s	c	u	e	j	h	u
m	e	s	s	a	g	e	f	r	z	a	i	e	r	r
e	K	i	j	u	f	t	r	h	b	j	l	o	e	b
u	y	p	m	a	r	y	e	s	l	k	o	v	n	v
y	h	r	d	e	s	w	s	b	g	a	e	o	p	t
h	e	o	i	n	a	K	l	a	a	r	t	v	c	b
j	g	m	s	a	w	n	z	o	o	b	i	u	g	K
y	o	i	i	b	h	p	i	f	l	y	y	r	d	a
l	K	s	u	t	o	p	e	l	e	K	i	d	h	w
a	l	e	e	w	o	t	a	q	a	v	x	c	u	n
i	j	l	f	p	s	u	n	s	z	t	b	m	h	o
c	i	o	p	h	h	b	g	r	h	f	a	v	K	s
e	t	r	b	m	l	o	e	g	j	t	i	c	i	i
p	b	y	d	r	e	p	l	l	y	u	f	g	n	l
s	u	e	d	r	e	a	m	v	e	x	i	o	g	a

The special star

The special star

Some wise men living far, far away had also been sent a message...

Can you find the special star that the wise men saw? Match the star in the telescope to the one in the sky, then decorate the picture.

Wordsearch 2

d	r	b	m	a	j	u	a	n	m	g	j	s	o	n
g	a	e	f	s	o	o	r	j	n	r	a	l	c	b
r	n	t	e	v	o	l	u	i	u	a	c	o	e	r
s	d	h	u	d	K	b	p	r	m	e	o	l	l	e
a	r	l	w	n	y	e	o	z	n	f	b	w	e	d
r	e	e	t	s	e	y	f	p	s	e	t	h	b	t
a	d	h	u	l	m	K	s	e	p	u	y	d	r	h
h	i	e	s	h	e	p	h	e	r	d	s	n	a	n
m	t	m	i	l	l	i	e	h	e	d	o	e	t	a
e	K	o	p	s	y	o	p	s	s	e	y	f	e	g
w	i	s	e	m	e	n	i	t	e	t	t	r	o	e
f	w	n	c	a	m	e	l	r	n	i	s	m	e	m
d	r	e	a	y	x	p	d	u	t	c	a	t	u	i
t	m	a	n	g	e	r	p	g	s	x	e	y	a	g
s	i	e	i	g	g	a	m	y	t	e	j	f	o	r

The greatest King

Now read the book!

If you enjoyed this activity book, check out the full story in "The Christmas Promise."

Also available: The Christmas Promise Advent Calendar and board book

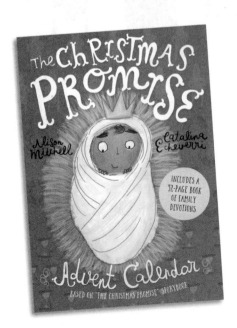

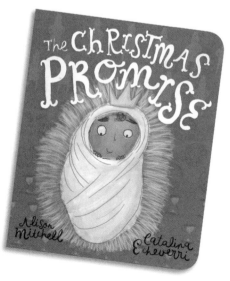

Other books available in the award-winning "Tales That Tell The Truth" series:

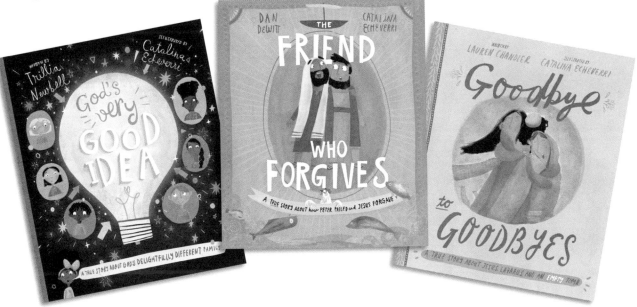

www.thegoodbook.com
www.thegoodbook.co.uk